M000187430

EVERGLADES

NATIONAL PARK

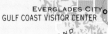

EVERGLADES CITY ○
GULF COAST VISITOR CENTER

BIG

TEN THOUSAND ISLANDS

Wilderness Water

CYPRESS

MARSH AND HAMMOCK

MANGROVE

PINELAND

GULF OF

MEXICO

Ponce de Leon Bay

BIG CYPRESS
NATIONAL PRESERVE

F L O R I D A

MIAMI

EVERGLADES
NATIONAL
PARK

*GULF OF
MEXICO*

*ATLANTIC
OCEAN*

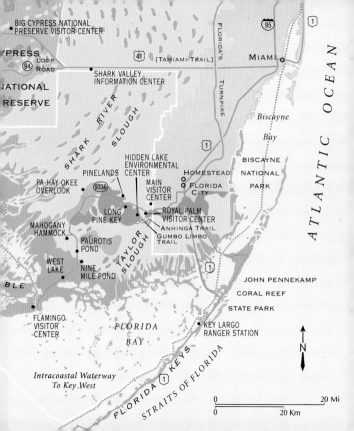

EVERGLADES

NATIONAL PARK

NATIONAL PARKS AND
CONSERVATION ASSOCIATION

———

Photographs by Patricia Caulfield
Text by Ted Levin

A TINY FOLIO™
Abbeville Press · Publishers
New York · London · Paris

FRONT COVER: Snowy egret. See page 157.
BACK COVER: Young alligator. See page 219.
SPINE: Roseate spoonbills. See page 177.

EDITOR: Susan Costello
DESIGNER: Celia Fuller
PRODUCTION EDITOR: Abigail Asher
PRODUCTION MANAGER: Lou Bilka
MAPS: Guenter Vollath

FIRST EDITION
1 3 5 7 9 10 8 6 4 2

Library of Congress Cataloging-in-Publication Data
Caulfield, Patricia.
Everglades National Park/National Parks and Conservation
Association ; photographs by Patricia Caulfield ; text by Ted Levin.
p. cm. — (A tiny folio)
Includes index.
ISBN 1-55859-827-8
1. Everglades National Park (Fla.) 2. Everglades National Park (Fla.)—
Pictorial works. 3. Natural history—Florida—Everglades National Park.
4. Natural history—Florida—Everglades National Park—Pictorial works.
I. Levin, Ted, 1948– . II. National Parks and Conservation Association.
III. Title. IV. Series: Tiny folios.
F317.E9C38 1995
917. 59′390463—dc20   94-46988

CONTENTS

PREFACE

by Paul C. Pritchard
President, National Parks and Conservation Association

The Florida Everglades is neither swamp nor mangrove forest nor water nor coastal wetlands—it is all of these things put together, and more.

The Everglades was first considered for protection as a park in the late 1920s. The National Parks and Conservation Association sent Frederick Law Olmsted, Jr., and William P. Wharton to study the area in 1931 to ensure that it was worthy of park status. They concluded that the Everglades' "primitive natural conditions" were of "national outstanding distinction" and recommended that preservation efforts proceed quickly because of the prospect of widespread destruction of wildlife and habitat. Everglades National Park was authorized by Congress in 1934.

But it was not until publication of Marjory Stoneman Douglas' *River of Grass* that the public began to recognize the Everglades' special value. Because of a new understanding of the area's rich diversity, efforts to designate the Everglades as a national park finally succeeded in 1947.

Since then, pollution and diversion of the Everglades' waters have caused severe problems for the fragile ecosystem. Wading bird populations have been nearly wiped out, and Florida panthers are on the brink of extinction. Everglades National Park is considered the most threatened of all the 368 units of the National Park System.

Today, we continue to learn about this exceptional place and to work toward restoring it—not just for native plants and wildlife, but for all humanity. This book will help you understand why Everglades National Park is so special.

FOREWORD
by Ted Levin

The Everglades waits for me. That's what I think on cold winter nights when trees moan and branches snap and heavy air falls like an anvil out of the north, pressing my heart to my toes. I can close my eyes in January, see alligators, heads barely above the surface, eyes unblinking, and rejoice in their kinship with antiquity and with the restlessness of cypress and sawgrass. Or, a gathering of egrets, poised and dignified, yellow eyes fixed on fish, waiting . . . . Like me. At my home in Vermont winter sets the seasonal agenda and I always seem to be getting ready for it. Order wood. Stack wood. Rake leaves. Mow lawn. Insulate crawl space, windows, doors. Put the garden to bed. Wake up snow tires, flannel shirts, long underwear and so on.

When my labors are done (or simply abandoned) the Everglades rises like a dream. Lures me. Down there, where the land is taut as Nebraska and ephemeral cloud-mountains congeal in the morning sun, expanding, contracting like a giant white Rorschach, you see and feel the great arch of the sky, watch big weather being born. You can stand in the Everglades and be pummeled by winds that passed over Cuba. At night frogs still grunt and croak and peep and chime, and in the cool darkness of a tropical hammock, an owl sends a love note; flowers still bloom. Behold, I wear a skirt of many colored birds, Florida seems to say to me.

Then, I come, arms wide, and embrace the American subtropics . . . . The Everglades . . . . For I need its wild, unpredictable nature as a tonic against the lethargy of winter, to remind me that I am alive.

THETFORD, VERMONT

INTRODUCTION

Everglades National Park encompasses a unique association of tropical and temperate plants and animals. Nowhere else in the United States can you find American crocodiles and West Indian manatees, snail kites and multicolored tree snails, which decorate trees like so many Christmas ornaments. Nowhere else in the United States does such a variety of orchids and bromeliads and ferns festoon the branches of wetland trees or do palm trees grow a hundred feet tall. Panthers and black bears still roam through stands of cypress and pine; bald eagles and ospreys and brown pelicans still fish the shallow salty waters of Florida Bay; and sea turtles still lumber up the pristine beaches of Cape Sable to lay their eggs.

On December 6, 1947 Harry S. Truman, the thirty-third president of the United States, dedicated the southern tip of Florida as Everglades National Park, the first park in the world to be protected for its biology rather than its awesome geologic scenery. In 1976 the United Nations declared the park an International Biosphere Reserve, three years later a World Heritage Site, and in 1987 a Wilderness of International Significance.

In earlier years the subtropical skies of the glades were filled with wading birds and the inland waters with alligators. Robert Porter Allen estimated that in the 1930s one and a half million wading birds nested in the mangroves between Rodgers River and Shark River and flew north to the edge of the sawgrass to feed, squalls of birds so large and white you'd have had to shield your eyes from the glare. No one knows for sure if that many ibis and herons and egrets really gathered in what is now Everglades National Park or if 100,000 alligators—the oft quoted number—actually lived there. What is generally accepted is this: waders and gators must have lived in the Everglades in extraordinary numbers to have generated those sorts of estimates. These animals were more than simply monster gene pools in a singular wetland; they were a phenomenon, a visual feast of numbing proportions, like the boundless plain of sawgrass itself. We need natural phenomena to nurture our spirit, numbers beyond counting, birds beyond belief.

The Everglades is the largest freshwater marsh in the United States and—unique among the Earth's great wetlands—is driven by rain and rain alone. There is no mountain range here that pours its waters toward the sea. No river that overflows its banks. As though adhering to a doctrine of simplicity, the Everglades begins as a cloud above central Florida, a wilderness born in the sky. The more it rains, the more it flows.

Once extending more than one hundred miles from Lake Okeechobee to the southern tip of the mainland, the Everglades alone covered more than 6,000 square miles, an area larger than the state of Connecticut. The entire watershed, which includes the Big Cypress, Lake Okeechobee, and Kissimmee River and extends north almost to Orlando, covers more than 13,000 square miles—and is still the principal feature of South Florida, a wide, shallow trough imperceptibly tilted at less than two inches per mile. You can stand all day rooted in one spot and never notice a current. FLAT is the operable word down here. Desktop flat like West Texas.

Rarely does water from the northern glades (or the occasional overflow from Lake Okeechobee) ever reach Florida Bay or the Gulf of Mexico; the sun and the vegetation would call it back—evaporating and transpiring—and return it to the clouds, where it would fall again as rain. And again . . . .

Hydrologically speaking, which is the only way to speak about wild South Florida, everything—Lake Okeechobee, the Atlantic Coastal Ridge, Big Cypress Swamp, the Everglades, the tangle of mangroves along the coast, even Florida Bay—is joined through the underlying porous limestone, where water and aquatic animals move through a subterranean maze of tunnels and caverns even though the marsh above may appear bone-dry. Subtle contours in the limestone translate into plant communities. Inches make a difference: the coastal ridge on the Atlantic side of the glades, broken only by a few transverse cuts, funnels water southward down the marsh and once supported a slash pine forest (now Florida's Gold Coast from Miami to Homestead). Grooves in the limestone three or four feet deep that fill with organic material support linear cypress and pond apple swamps and are called *strands;* epidermal grooves, wide, long, and shallow—the main channels in the Everglades—are called *sloughs:* they support water lilies, pickerel weed, and bladderwort, and curve through nearly level fields of sawgrass, sawgrass as far as the eye can see (and then some); bumps in the limestone that rise above water level support jungles of tropical hardwood trees and are called *hammocks*. In some areas mats of peat called *heads* have bubbled up from the bottom and are colonized by red bay, cocoplum, or coastal plain willow. Collectively, these communities form a green tapestry, a diverse and alluring landscape, whose very name, Everglades, conjures images of the untamed and unknown, an American original.

Geography, too, plays a key role in defining the Everglades. Situated at the end of a long, temperate peninsula, South Florida is surrounded by warm, shallow seawater and bathed by tropical weather. There are two seasons down here: wet and dry. Although it may rain every month of the year, 80 percent of the yearly rainfall usually comes between May and November, when the weather resembles a steam bath. Then, thunderstorms convene in the broad afternoon sky, casting sheets of rain and firing bolts of lightning that often ignite patches of marsh and pine (both communities are fire-dependent). Watch the cumulus clouds rise thousands of feet into the blue; they are so common, people call them "Florida's mountains." Ephemeral, malleable, spectacular, they orchestrate lavish sunsets.

South Florida's plants and animals must tolerate wind. Tropical cyclones—storms with circular winds greater than thirty-nine mph—have struck the Everglades so often that plant communities have been shaped by their passage. Seeds are dispersed. Trees are toppled or stripped of leaves, branches, and bark. No place in the United States has been slammed by more hurricanes (tropical cyclones with winds greater than seventy-four mph) than peninsular Florida.

Florida lures most visitors in winter, during the dry season. Except for the occasional broad frontal system that covers the entire eastern seaboard, bringing days of rain and cool temperatures to the Everglades, the dry season is marked by clear skies, low humidity, and warmth. Everything begins to cure then. And, as the shallow marshes bake beneath the mass of the subtropical sun, fish, frogs, turtles, snakes, alligators, and wading birds are corralled into smaller and smaller pockets of water, often into "holes" dug by the gators themselves.

The start of either season, however, is not always predictable. Drought may last for several years, and then in some years it seems never to stop raining. To survive down here plants and animals must adjust to the whims of the weather. For some species of birds, amphibians, and plants, water levels trigger behavior. Yet every month of the year a bird breeds, a frog sings, a flower blooms.

The very same year Everglades National Park was dedicated by President Truman, federal and state agencies were busy dismantling the broad, shallow sheet of water that defines the region. Locks, levees, floodgates, dikes, and canals were constructed to either divert or impound water. In the 1950s the Kissimmee River, the principal tributary that feeds Lake Okeechobee, was transformed from a meandering hundred-mile-long river into a fifty-mile long channel, C-38. South of the lake the northern Everglades region, once covered with sawgrass ten feet tall, now grows 700,000 acres of sugar cane and sundry vegetables and is called the Everglades Agricultural Area, the watershed's leading source of phosphorus pollution. South Florida's more than four million residents tax both the surface water and the aquifers. Exotic trees like melaleuca and Brazilian pepper and exotic fish like walking catfish and tilapia have staked out niches and thrive at the expense of native plants and animals. Mercury courses through the wetlands, through the bass and raccoons, and no one knows where it comes from. The population of wading birds has crashed in fifty years, and only a monumental effort by federal and state biologists and private land owners will rescue the Florida panther from extinction.

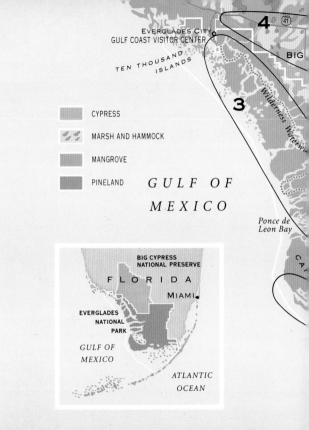

EVERGLADES CITY
GULF COAST VISITOR CENTER

TEN THOUSAND ISLANDS

4 ㊶

BIG

Wilderness Waterway

3

CYPRESS

MARSH AND HAMMOCK

MANGROVE

PINELAND

G U L F   O F

M E X I C O

Ponce de Leon Bay

CA

BIG CYPRESS
NATIONAL PRESERVE

F L O R I D A

MIAMI

EVERGLADES
NATIONAL
PARK

*GULF OF
MEXICO*

*ATLANTIC
OCEAN*

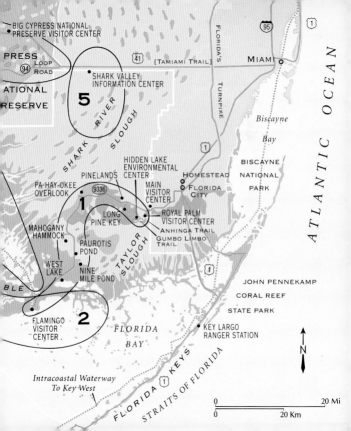

The map on pages 18–19 shows the Everglades's four distinctive habitats. The beige swath punctuated by gray "teardrops" is the marshland, or Everglades, a vast, slow moving "river of grass." The teardrops are hammocks, outcrops of limestone, which have been colonized by tropical hardwoods and tapered at their southern ends by the slow, persistent movement of water. Other islands, bayheads and willowheads, pepper the Everglades and are named for their dominant vegetation. Within the marshland are sloughs, ponds, sawgrass, and wet prairies, each ordered by its respective hydroperiod (the time during which the soil is water-logged).

The pinelands, dark green on the map, grow on ridges of limestone that remain above water most of the year. Without fire, the slash pine forests revert to hardwoods. Hammocks grow in the pinelands in areas protected from fire and contribute to the pinelands' great diversity of plants.

Cypress, brown on the map, grow in depressions in the limestone and have longer hydroperiods than marsh plants. West of the Everglades is a vast shallow basin, the Big Cypress Swamp, named not for the size of its trees but for its extent. Potholes in the southern glades support rounded islands of cypress called domes.

Mangroves, green on the map, grow in brackish zones where freshwater from the Everglades and the Big Cypress meets the salt water of the gulf and Florida Bay coasts. Named for three species of unrelated trees, this is the most biologically productive region in Florida.

That effort, however, is underway for the panther as well as for the entire watershed from the Kissim-mee River to Florida Bay, the largest ecological restoration ever undertaken on Earth, the corner-stone of the Clinton administration's "whole system" approach to managing our nation's natural resources. Everglades National Park and Big Cypress National Preserve will benefit from the effort as biologists, hydrologists, engineers, politicians, naturalists, artists, educators, and farmers work together to keep the glass bells ringing.

This "tiny folio" celebrates the wildness and beauty of the Everglades and Big Cypress Swamp. Photographs are organized in three sections: First, the scenic section covers five tours a visitor is likely to take by boat or car or on foot. The next sections are devoted to the region's animals and plants, arranged taxonomically.

SCENIC TOURS

The photographs in Section 1, the *Scenics,* are grouped into five discrete areas or tours, each accompanied by a map and caption that will alert you to places of interest: routes, trails, boardwalks, observation towers, and so on. Tour 1 is the main road in Everglades National Park from the Homestead/Florida City entrance to Flamingo. This road has been called "thirty-eight miles of nothing," but that is far off the mark; passing by every major habitat, including fire-shaped and fire-excluded pinelands, and for the first fifteen miles following the path of Hurricane Andrew (notice the fallen and broken pines and wind-thinned canopies of roadside hammocks), it is a splendid introduction to the subtleties of South Florida topography. A road sign at mile 12 announces Rock Reef Pass, elevation three feet. This narrow ridge of limestone "rises" above the adjacent sawgrass marsh and supports a serpentine line of woody vegetation. Barely noticeable

Spring flowers brighten a sea of grass.

from the ground, Rock Reef Pass separates Shark River Slough from Taylor Slough, the two major drainages of the Everglades.

Tour 2 is Florida Bay and Cape Sable. Larger than the state of Delaware, Florida Bay has an average depth of four feet and a maximum depth of nine feet. At low tide marl flats extend from the shorelines of the approximately one hundred islets, or mangrove keys, that dot the bay and convene clouds of shorebirds, terns, and gulls. The beaches of Cape Sable, which are the finest in Everglades National Park, are made of pulverized shell and every summer incubate the eggs of loggerhead sea turtles. When water levels in the Everglades are high, a plume of freshwater from Shark River Slough flows around the gulf side of Cape Sable and enters the northwest corner of Florida Bay.

Tour 3 is the Wilderness Waterway from Everglades City to Flamingo, including the Ten Thousand Island district of Everglades National Park. Within this section you may be more than twenty-five miles from the nearest road, which makes it the largest roadless area in the lower forty-eight states.

Tour 4 is, for the most part, the southern half of Big Cypress National Preserve and nearby Fakahatchee

Strand State Preserve. The pop ash and pond apple sloughs in Fakahatchee support the greatest diversity of orchids in North America: thirty-eight species, seven of which are found nowhere else in the United States.

Tour 5 is the northern portion of Everglades National Park known as Shark Valley. During wet years, like the fall of 1994, Shark Valley may be underwater, as Shark River Slough rises and spreads across road and parking area. During drought years, when only the roadside canal holds water, the sawgrass may be dry and brown as a South Dakota prairie.

Within each tour pictures are arranged systematically, as a natural progression that a visitor would follow by either car or boat or on foot. One or more aerials opens each section, followed by specific places and habitats along the route. Photographs of common species of animals and plants that are associated with a particular region and that a visitor would likely see—alligators on the Anhinga Trail, Tour 1, for instance—are included with the groupings in the Scenics Section. Most of the picture locations, which are listed in the accompanying captions, can be found on the area map or within the broad range of the habitat map on pages 18 and 19.

MAIN PARK ROAD

The main park road in Everglades National Park runs thirty-eight miles from the Homestead/Florida City entrance southwest to Flamingo. The Visitor Center, just beyond the entrance station, is an excellent starting point. The most popular site in the park is Royal Palm Hammock, where you can watch wildlife from the Anhinga Trail boardwalk or follow the Gumbo Limbo Trail through a tropical hardwood hammock. The Pineland Trail, seven miles from the entrance station, loops through slash pine forest, a community that depends on wildfire. At mile 12.5, the observation platform at Pa-hay-okee Overlook rises above the sawgrass. For the more adventurous, a short, wet bushwhack off the Pa-hay-okee access road into a cypress dome can be memorable. The boardwalk at Mahogany Hammock, mile 19.5, winds through a West Indian hardwood forest that contains the largest living mahogany tree in the United States (page 263). Several miles south of Mahogany Hammock the road enters brackish zone vegetation, which continues all the way to Flamingo on Florida Bay. The short boardwalk at West Lake, mile 30.5, passes through a mangrove forest (be sure to scan the open water for an American crocodile). Farther south, the Snake Bight Trail, mile 32.7, and the Christian Point trail, mile 36.6, lead to Florida Bay, where shorebirds and wading birds gather at low tide.

Aerial view of sawgrass prairie, a vast sea of grass and sedges
punctuated by hardwood hammocks, or "islands of trees."

Located near the main visitor entrance, Anhinga Trail is the most popular site in the National Park. The trail offers views of wildlife, including a large population of its namesake bird during the winter, breeding months.

An alligator floats in the canal adjacent to Anhinga Trail as a great egret pauses in its search for small fish and frogs to eat.

Dade County slash pine is a medium-sized tree that once covered huge tracts in south Florida. The largest remaining stands are now in Everglades National Park.

The Pinelands Trail, located off the Main Park Road, winds through pine and hardwood hammocks.

ABOVE AND OPPOSITE. Saw palmettos, the principal understory on the pinelands, is favored by wildfire.

Rock Reef Pass, a snaking ridge of limestone, is only four feet above sea level, a veritable mountain by Everglades' standards.

Male flowers, or tassels of the cypress, one of the four
evergreens that shed their needles, near the Pa-Hay-Okee
(a Seminole term for "grassy waters") Overlook.

ABOVE. Mahogany hammock is a tropical forest similar
to those in the Greater Antilles.
OPPOSITE. A great blue heron stands still in the natural moat
that surrounds a mahogany hammock.

ABOVE AND OPPOSITE. Paurotis Pond at sunset.

Nine Mile Pond, an estuary, is rimmed by mangroves.

West Lake, mid-morning, is home to rare
American crocodiles.

A snowy egret in Mrazek Pond.

Clouds drift over Coot Bay Pond, which was named for the
birds that once frequented them in such numbers that
the water is said to have been carpeted.

A wedge of cattails along the edge of Eco Pond.

A common moorhen in Eco Pond.

Everglades sunsets are kaleidoscopic.

CAPE SABLE AND FLORIDA BAY

Except for the Coastal Prairie Trail, which starts at the campground in Flamingo and leads west to Clubhouse Beach, you need a boat to explore Cape Sable and Florida Bay. If the trade winds are light, Florida Bay by canoe (which can be rented at the Flamingo Marina) will put you in proximity to shorebirds, terns, gulls, and pelicans, particularly at low tide. Canoeing into Snake Bight or around the marl flats off Joe Kemp are easy day trips. If the wind is too strong to paddle the open bay, head up the Buttonwood Canal from the marina into Coot Bay or portage over to the Bear Lake Canoe Trail. Strong canoeists can follow the Bear Lake Trail to East Cape Canal, which enters the Gulf of Mexico at East Cape Sable, about three miles west of Clubhouse Beach. Back country camping is permitted on the beach at Clubhouse, East Cape, Middle Cape, and Northwest Cape on Cape Sable and on Little Rabbit Key in Florida Bay. If you prefer a less strenuous outing but still want the joy of wilderness camping, the Flamingo Marina provides drop-off and pickup service to Cape Sable, as well as birding tours in Florida Bay.

Above. Florida Bay, shallow and tidal, is cut by
natural channels.
Opposite. Isles in Florida Bay are called keys.

ABOVE AND OPPOSITE. The "walking trees," red mangroves, have prop roots that rise like spider legs from the water.

PAGES 56–57. The peace and tranquillity of Florida Bay.

Above. Tern chick on Cape Sable.
Opposite. The sweep of Cape Sable beach and the attendant
Gulf of Mexico.

59

Prickly pear cactus thrive on Cape Sable.

Spanish bayonet, a yucca, on Cape Sable.

WILDERNESS WATERWAY

Everglades City is the launch site for a visit to the Ten Thousand Islands, a jig-saw puzzle of mangrove isles, and for the Wilderness Waterway. Recommended for canoeists and small power boats, the Wilderness Waterway is a hundred-mile marked boat trail through mangrove-lined creeks, rivers, lagoons, and open bays, which ends (or begins) in Flamingo.

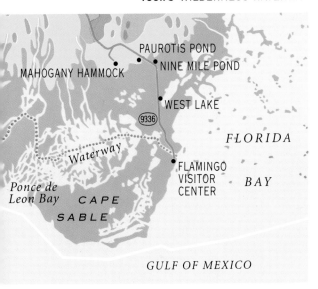

Narrow channels and overhanging vegetation make this route hazardous to boats over eighteen feet or those with high cabins. Camping on the Wilderness Waterway or in the Ten Thousand Islands is restricted to designated sites. The Turner River Canoe Trail, which begins on the Tamiami Trail, east of State Road 839, and ends on Chokoloskee Island, is an excellent day trip.

PAGES 64–65. The mangrove-lined Harney River empties into the Gulf of Mexico.

Above. Ten Thousand Islands, a maze of mangroves and
salt water.

Above and opposite. Flocks of birds gather in the shallows
of the Ten Thousand Islands.
Pages 70–71. A channel in the Wilderness Waterway,
accessible only at high tide.

The breathing roots of black mangroves rise from
the shoreline.

Roseate spoonbills against a wall of mangroves.

Black skimmers and shorebirds at rest on a beach in the
Ten Thousand Islands.

Royal terns perch on a red mangrove tree.

Terns, gulls, oystercatchers, and shorebirds rise from a
sand spit.

Above and pages 78–79. White ibis returning to their roost
in the Ten Thousand Islands.

BIG CYPRESS NATIONAL PRESERVE

The Oasis Visitor Center on the Tamiami Trail (US 41), twenty-one miles east of State Road (S.R.) 29, is the starting point for hiking Big Cypress National Preserve; more than forty miles of hiking trails extend north to Alligator Alley (U.S. 75) and south to Loop Road (S.R. 94). There are five primitive campgrounds along the Tamiami Trail and two along the Loop Road. Tent camping on the hiking trails is allowed anywhere you can find high ground. Bring your own water. The Loop Road (S.R. 94) runs twenty-four miles from Forty Mile Bend to Monroe Station, much of it unimproved. An early morning bicycle ride is often rewarded by sightings of barred owl, otter, wild turkey, and bobcat. The Turner River Road, an eighteen-mile graded dirt road, connects the Tamiami Trail at H.P. Williams Roadside Park to Alligator Alley. Look for wading birds in the roadside canal. W. J. Janes Scenic Drive, an eleven-mile gravel road off S.R. 29 in Copeland, crosses Fakahatchee Strand State Preserve, the western end of the Big Cypress Swamp. Fakahatchee is the least visited state-owned land in Florida. There are no facilities. Twenty old logging roads, called trams, intersect Janes Drive and are marked by gates that prevent vehicular traffic. Six trams have been cleared for walking. Gate 7, the most scenic, is 4.4 miles from headquarters and passes through

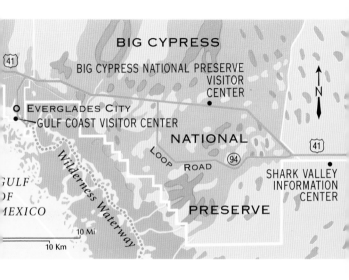

cypress strands and hardwood hammock before opening onto Four Stakes Prairie. Look for airplants and royal palms, panther tracks and shredded cabbage palms where black bears have fed on the hearts of palm.

81

ABOVE. Spring wildfire in Big Cypress.

PAGES 82–83. Big Cypress National Preserve in winter.

Fire in the pines.

Interior of a cypress stand.

White ibis roosting in cypress.

Above. Gnarled roots of pop ash.
Opposite. Pop ash and pond apple trees.

Buttress cypress rises from watery soil.

ABOVE. Cypress knees.
PAGES 92–93. The Turner River winds south toward the
Ten Thousand Islands.

Above. A carpet of spring flowers.
Opposite. Cypress dome and wetland flowers.

Cabbage palm and palm islands.

A black-necked stilt feigning a broken wing.

Lostman's pines in the Big Cypress National Preserve.

Sunset over Big Cypress.

SHARK VALLEY

Shark Valley, the northern entrance to Everglades National Park, is on the Tamiami Trail eighteen miles west of the intersection of Krome Avenue (S.R. 997). The Information Center offers educational exhibits and programs. A fifteen-mile loop road (Tram Road) leads to a sixty-five-foot observation tower. The road crosses Shark River Slough, the principal drainage of the Everglades, and is eight miles long on the meandering east side. The engineer-straight west side of the loop parallels a canal where alligators and wading birds are easy to see. Although only authorized motor vehicles are allowed on the road, the concession operates narrated tram tours. The loop is a leisurely two-hour bicycle ride, best in early morning when deer are grazing in the marsh and otter are gamboling in the water. If you are on foot, follow the canal; there is more wildlife to see. The Bobcat Trail, 0.25 miles, crosses a bayhead and bridges the two legs of the Tram Road near the parking area. The Otter Trail, a one-mile path through a hammock, starts on the west leg of the loop a half mile from the visitor center. A spur trail near the base of the observation tower, called the Tower Trail, follows the canal for 0.25 miles. The tower itself offers the park's best panorama of the Everglades as well as excellent opportunities to watch alligators, turtles, herons, egrets, anhingas, and cormorants. Occasionally, snail kites are spotted from the tower or above the Tram Road.

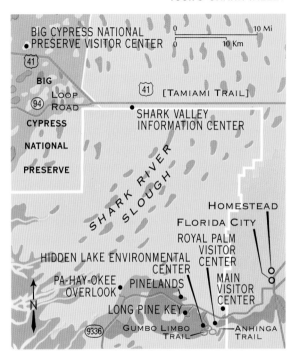

BIG CYPRESS NATIONAL
PRESERVE VISITOR CENTER

0 · · · · · · 10 Mi
0 · · · · · · 10 Km

41

BIG

94 LOOP
ROAD

41 [TAMIAMI TRAIL]

CYPRESS

SHARK VALLEY
INFORMATION CENTER

NATIONAL

PRESERVE

SHARK RIVER SLOUGH

HOMESTEAD

FLORIDA CITY

ROYAL PALM
VISITOR
CENTER

HIDDEN LAKE ENVIRONMENTAL
CENTER

MAIN
VISITOR
CENTER

PA-HAY-OKEE
OVERLOOK · PINELANDS

LONG PINE KEY

N

9336 GUMBO LIMBO
TRAIL

ANHINGA
TRAIL

The sixty-five-foot-high Shark Valley observation tower and tram.

Alligators in pool below the Shark Valley tower.

ABOVE. Glossy ibis rise from a pool.
OPPOSITE. An alligator drifting like a log.

Blades of sawgrass rise from periphyton, an algae mat.

Yellow bladderwort in a slough.

Semi-aquatic whitetail deer.

A doe and a fawn in sawgrass.

WILDLIFE

The photographs in this section are arranged in scientific order by animal group—mammals, birds, reptiles and amphibians, fish, and invertebrates—and within each group by species. Many animals shown here are common and are fairly easy to see, particularly the wading birds, while others, like the coral snake, are secretive. A few, like the Florida panther, are endangered and elusive. The snail kite, bald eagle, manatee, and American crocodile are also federally listed as endangered species, but their haunts are usually predictable.

Diligence and patience are your allies. Look for snail kites around Shark Valley; observe bald eagles above Florida Bay (sometimes from the breezeway in Flamingo) or in the pines near Mahogany Hammock, where the juveniles roost. Manatees are often spotted from the concession boat cruise in Chokoloskee Bay; and American crocodiles may be found basking on the bank of the Buttonwood Canal.

Most species of mammals are active at dusk and dawn. Search for bobcat and gray fox crossing the main park road around Flamingo. Eyeshine, the eerie light reflected back from an animal's eyes, is an excellent way to spot nocturnal animals. Most mammals have yellow or green eyeshine; whippoorwills orange; alligators and crocodiles red; and wolf spiders blue.

None of the four species of venomous snakes in the region is aggressive. As a precaution, however, watch where you place your feet. The eastern diamondback rattlesnake, which can be up to seven feet long, is the largest and the pygmy rattlesnake, about two feet long, the smallest. Do not molest them; to see one is a thrill. Look for diamondbacks and pygmies in the pinelands; moccasins (cottonmouths) sun on cypress knees and on any natural or artificial berm adjacent to freshwater. Coral snakes hide beneath rotting logs and fallen leaves.

Although alligators are associated with freshwater and crocodiles with salt water, both species coexist in the brackish mangrove zone at the mouth of Taylor Slough. Every week to ten days, a large gator leaves Eco Pond, walks across the Flamingo campground—to the delight of everyone—enters Florida Bay, and swims northeast to the marina, where it scavenges fish guts near the boat dock. Please enjoy gators from a safe distance and do NOT feed them (or any other wildlife).

Above. A bellowing alligator.
Page 110. A bobcat in buttonwood.

ABOVE AND OPPOSITE. An opossum on a limb.

PAGES 116–117. Nine-banded armadillo, an alien mammal.

ABOVE AND OPPOSITE. Mangrove fox squirrel.
PAGES 120–21. Florida black bear in a pine forest.

ABOVE AND OPPOSITE. Foraging raccoon at the edge of
Mrazek Pond.

ABOVE AND OPPOSITE. River otter, making a game of life.

Florida panther in saw palmetto.

Young panther in the Big Cypress.

ABOVE AND OPPOSITE. Bobcat, a short-tailed, tuft-eared relative of the lynx, is common in the glades.

PAGES 130–31. Whitetailed deer camouflaged in sawgrass in winter.

ABOVE AND OPPOSITE. Fawn in a sawgrass prairie.

ABOVE AND OPPOSITE. Manatees, or sea cows.
PAGE 136–37. An Atlantic bottle-nosed dolphin leaping.

Brown pelicans cruising above the treetops.

ABOVE. Pelican rookery, also inhabited by
double-crested cormorants.
PAGES 140–41. An anhinga (on the left) and a
double-crested cormorant.

Male anhinga preening.

Female anhingas in water.

American bittern, a winter visitor.

Great blue heron stalking.

Great blue heron flying.

Great blue heron landing.

Portrait of an adult great blue heron.

Hungry great blue heron chicks.

Portrait of a great white heron.

Great white heron preening.

ABOVE: Great white heron stretching in Florida Bay.
OPPOSITE: Great egret, symbol of the National
Audubon Society.

ABOVE: A snowy egret hunting in Eco Pond.
OPPOSITE: An assemblage of snowy egrets at Mrazek Pond.

A dance of egrets.

Snowy egret in breeding finery.

ABOVE AND OPPOSITE. Snowy egrets at Mrazek Pond.

A snowy egret at Mrazek Pond.

Snowy egrets dispute a feeding site.

ABOVE: Green-backed heron waiting for prey in
shallow waters.
OPPOSITE: Green-backed heron chicks.

Tricolored heron hunting.

Above: Tricolored heron feeding in the shallows.
Opposite: Tricolored heron strikes.

Pages 168–169. Near the Anhinga Trail: a tricolored heron, aided by its long, pointed bill, can pluck a morsel from a pond with great speed.

Opposite and Above: Cattle heron rookery.

Black-crowned night heron, hunching.

Yellow-crowned night heron, stretching.

White ibis, the essence of the Everglades.

Immature white ibis at Eco Pond.

ABOVE. A gathering of a roseate spoonbill and white
ibis at Eco Pond.
OPPOSITE. Roseate spoonbills feed at Mrazek Pond.
PAGES 178–79. A roseate spoonbill at sunrise.

Black vultures gather at a large fish kill.

Turkey vultures at a road kill.

Above. Osprey at home along the Wilderness Waterway.
Opposite. Osprey chicks above a coastal prairie.

Snail kite feeding on escargot (above)
and soaring (opposite).

ABOVE AND OPPOSITE. Bald eagle.

Above. Red-shouldered hawk.
Opposite. Red-shouldered hawk soaring over Eco Pond.

Purple gallinule, long-toed and gaudy.

Wild turkeys.

ABOVE. An American coot dispute at Eco Pond.
OPPOSITE. Common moorhen.

Limpkin searching for apple snails.

Sandhill cranes.

Above. Black-necked stilts perching on their nest.
Opposite. A convocation at high tide of royal terns,
American oystercatchers, and ruddy turnstones.

ABOVE. A mosaic of black skimmers.
OPPOSITE. Black skimmers and laughing gulls rest on a boat
ramp at high tide.

Mourning dove.

Smooth-billed ani at Eco Pond.

ABOVE. Young great horned owl.
OPPOSITE. The great horned owl, an adept night hunter.

ABOVE. A Northern cardinal on Eco Pond.
OPPOSITE. Barred owls, the most common owls in
the Everglades.

The ubiquitous and noisy red-winged blackbird.

Boat-tailed grackle in Shark Valley.

ABOVE AND OPPOSITE. Although rare and endangered, American crocodiles may be seen near Flamingo.

American alligators walking through the grass (above) and across Anhinga Trail (opposite).

ABOVE AND OPPOSITE. Alligators have round snouts while crocodiles have long, narrow snouts.

PAGES 214–15. An alligator swimming with its dinner.

Alligators in spring bellow mating calls.

Basking alligators.

ABOVE. Baby alligators colored like the shadowed marsh.
OPPOSITE. A young alligator reaches a length of three feet
between four and six years of age.

An alligator approaching a mangrove snake (above), and a Florida redbelly turtle (opposite).

221

Above. Hatchling snapping turtle.
Opposite. Florida redbelly turtle.

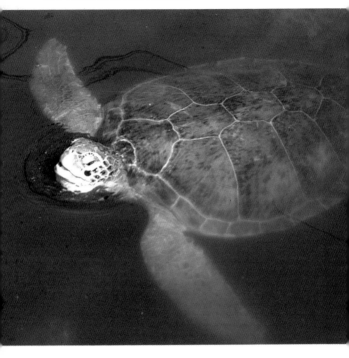

An Atlantic green turtle coming to the surface for air.

The Florida softshell turtle in a freshwater pond.

ABOVE AND OPPOSITE. Carolina anole.

Eastern hognose snake.

ABOVE. Yellow rat snake on slash pine.
PAGES 230–31, Yellow rat snakes entwined.

ABOVE. Yellow rat snake.
OPPOSITE. Coral snake, known for its beauty and venom.

A coral snake.

A baby cottonmouth.

Eastern diamondback rattlesnake swimming (opposite)
and in a threatening posture (above).

Green tree frogs have a white stripe along their sides.

Pig frogs have pointed snouts and piglike grunts.

Above. Largemouth bass, a popular sport fish.
Opposite. The Florida gar, a freshwater fish with an
ancient lineage.

Walking catfish, a South American exotic.

Leaping tarpon in Florida Bay.

Above. Eastern lubber grasshopper, large, flightless,
and almost always hungry.
Opposite. Halloween pennant dragonfly.

A female katydid prepares to lay her eggs on a pickerelweed.

Dung beetle in Big Cypress.

A sulphur butterfly emerging from its chrysalis.

Zebra butterflies return to semipermanent roosts at night.

ABOVE. Golden orb weaver.
OPPOSITE. Spiny orb weaver, an elegant small spider.

ABOVE AND OPPOSITE. Different color varieties of tree snails.

PLANTS

The photographs in this section begin with trees, followed with ferns, and end with wildflowers. Like greater Miami, the flora of the Everglades is multicultural. Of the more than 1,600 species of vascular plants (ferns and seed plants) in South Florida, 61 percent have tropical affinities, mostly from the Caribbean. Often in proximity, one can find the familiar—mulberry, red maple, live oak, wild grape, poison ivy, and persimmon—and the strange—strangler fig, poisonwood, West Indian mahogany, gumbo limbo, and paurotis palm; plants whose entire U.S. range is restricted to the southern tip of Florida.

Trade winds, birds, and ocean currents probably freighted the seeds of Caribbean species across the Straits of Florida. The seeds of the red mangrove,

---

Bald cypress needles

which looks like a great woody spider, legs raised and ready to walk, germinate on the tree, producing thin, tapered seedlings. Although hurricanes destroy old mangrove forests, they also disperse seedlings (propagules), hurling them like darts toward new mud-bank targets. The standing dead mangroves you see from the foot trails near Flamingo were killed in 1960 by Hurricane Donna and now support ospreys and vultures on their wizened gray limbs.

Two species of trees to avoid touching are poisonwood and manchineel. Sap of both species causes severe skin rashes. Poisonwood (pages 268–269) has alternate, compound leaves, and scaly reddish brown bark flecked with black spots, and grows in hammocks and pinelands, often on the edge of trails. Manchineel, which grows in brackish swamps and coastal hammocks, has simple, light green leaves, finely serrated, and fruit that resembles small, green apples. White-crowned pigeons relish the small yellowish fruit of poisonwood and consequently spread their seeds.

Sometimes the most important element in an ecosystem is the one found in least concentration. Sawgrass, the most abundant freshwater plant in the Everglades, the one responsible for the image "a river of grass," is not a grass at all but a sedge that thrives in a nutrient-poor environment, which ecologists call *oligotrophic.* The addition of nutrients encourages species whose presence had been restricted by the lack of phosphorous. When fertilizer-rich farm runoff enters the Everglades, exotic blooms of cattails replace sawgrass, which is less competitive, changing the very structure and function of the marsh. Fortunately, five farmland runoff filtration marshes totalling 40,000 acres will be built in the sugarcane fields north of the park to eliminate much of the alien phosphorus that has been coursing through the Everglades.

ABOVE. Ferns on buttressed base of cypress.
OPPOSITE. Spanish moss drapes the tops of the bald cypress.

ABOVE. Cabbage palm frond along a pinelands trail at Long Pine Key.
OPPOSITE. A paurotis palm planted near the beginning of the Anhinga Trail.

ABOVE. Saw palmetto grows in pinelands as understory.
OPPOSITE. This giant mahogany, on the boardwalk of a
mahogany hammock, is the largest in the United States and
is about 500 years old.

Strangler fig, an epiphytic parasite.

Fruit of short-leaf fig.

Gumbo limbo bark.

A strangler fig on a mahogany tree.

ABOVE AND OPPOSITE. Poisonwood is a tree-sized relative of poison ivy, and its sap may cause a skin irritation. Its growth is larger in hammocks than in pinelands and on roadsides. Beware of this tree throughout the Everglades and Big Cypress.

Introduced from Brazil, this exotic tree, the Brazilian pepper, was originally planted as an ornamental but has since invaded native plant communities. Its leaves cause a skin rash.

Berries on the dahoon, a small tree found in woodlands, swamps, and hammock edges.

ABOVE. The papaya tree is an exotic, widespread through the Everglades and Big Cypress.
OPPOSITE. This young red mangrove illustrates why the plant is also known as the walking mangrove.

ABOVE. Leather ferns are the largest American fern,
reaching up to twelve feet.
OPPOSITE. Resurrection ferns have fronds that dry up
and look dead during the long Everglades dry season. With
a rain the fronds flesh out, turn green, and look very
much alive.

Fiddleheads unfold to form new leaves on all fern species;
this is a leatherfern.

The bird nest fern grows in some of the larger Everglades hammocks and in stands in the Big Cypress.

ABOVE. Shelf fern on the Gumbo Limbo Trail.
OPPOSITE. Bracken ferns grow abundantly in hammocks, pinelands, and palmetto areas in full sun or part shade.

Water lily, a striking aquatic blossom.

Jack-in-the-pulpit.

As its name suggests, butterfly weed's brightly colored blossoms attract butterflies. This flower may be found along roadsides in dry soil.

Capable of reseeding itself, the beach sunflower, found in the Everglades area, can move up to fifty feet from its original bed.

Another hearty roadside inhabitant, the Canada thistle produces numerous blooms in summer.

Sabatias, daisylike pink flowers of several species, are much in evidence in the pinelands and prairies of the Big Cypress. 285

Prickly pear cactus flower in sandy soil on Cape Sable.

Glazed lobelia.

ABOVE. Bromeliads, relatives of pineapples, are epiphytes
or airplants.
OPPOSITE. Flower of a bromeliad.

Morning glories, above and opposite, are commonly seen in
hammocks and have flourished particularly since the
disturbances associated with Hurricane Andrew in 1992.

Sawgrass is the plant that gave the system its common
name, Everglades, and the poetic "river of grass."

The white-bracted sedge is frequently found in moist pinelands.

Yellow flag (above) and southern blue flag (opposite),
members of the iris family, brighten marshy habitats of the
Everglades. Sometimes these irises form sizable colonies on
the edges of marshlands.

Bladderwort is an aquatic plant found in ponds.

This wetlands-loving lily dwells on the sawgrass prairie.

A member of the amaryllis family, the swamp lily is a familiar flower in the region, blooming periodically throughout the year.

Showy spider lilies, whose species name means "fragrant lily," grow along the road in the sawgrass prairies, throughout the glades, and in Big Cypress.

A rose mallow is a wild hibiscus.

Butterfly orchid, one of the most widespread orchids in
the Everglades.

The flower of a pond apple tree has distinctive crimson markings.

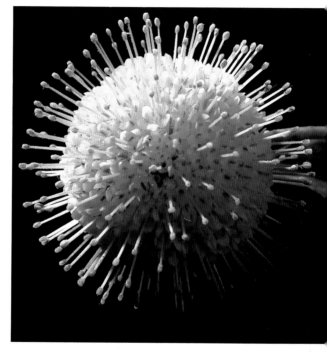

Buttonbush, an aquatic shrub.

ABOVE. Blue-eyed grass.
OPPOSITE. Lizard's tail growing in swamps.

TRAVEL TIPS

Most tourists visit south Florida during the November-to-April dry season, when the skies are usually clear and blue, the days warm, and the waters inviting. There is a possibility that the weather may not be fair. Arctic cold fronts do occasionally descend on the Everglades. Ice may temporarily seal pools, frost may singe the leaves of tropical trees and send cold-blooded animals into hiding, and snow may dust the sawgrass. As a matter of fact, these rare fronts have shaped the distribution and growing pattern of the tropical flora. So when you arrive at the doorstep of the Everglades make sure you pack a warm jacket and hat. Besides, if you're camping on the edge of Florida Bay, the wind can be relentless, chilling out an otherwise warm evening.

There are two other items that the prudent traveler should bring along: sunscreen and protection against insects. Although biting insects—mosquitoes, no-see-ums (sand flies), deer flies, and horse flies—have aquatic larva and are more often associated with the

rainy season, winter storms may translate into a hatch

of mosquitoes, particularly around Flamingo. You could be luxuriating in shirt sleeves and shorts in Shark Valley and then be driven to distraction when you arrive at Flamingo. While bug repellent holds insects at bay, DEET, the active ingredient in most repellents, is absorbed by the skin, has been linked to seizures and deaths, and dissolves vinyl and plastic, which renders binoculars and cameras sticky. Loosefitting, long-sleeved shirts, long pants, and a head net are safer and, particularly in summer in the mangroves, a prerequisite. If you must spray repellent, it is recommended that you spray your clothes, not your skin.

You may take some comfort in knowing that mosquito larvae are vital members of the aquatic food pyramid, upon whose pinnacle reside alligators and wading birds, and that only adult females bite. They need protein-rich blood to produce eggs. Nectar-feeding males, which look and act like harmless midges, are important pollinators of marsh flowers. So remember, should a mosquito penetrate your defenses, that you have "given in the Everglades," and for a worthy cause, too.

Please drive carefully: in winter snakes warm themselves on dark roads in the late afternoon; during heavy rain, animals move to high ground, which is often roadsides; and panthers and black bears cross both the Tamiami Trail and S.R. 29. Most mornings crows and vultures are on the Main Park Road scavenging the previous night's roadkills.

Everglades National Park provides seventy-five recycling bins for aluminum, glass, and plastic, located at the Shark Valley, Flamingo, and main visitor centers, as well as in campgrounds and picnic areas. Florida state parks provide bins for glass. So please sort your trash and wait for a recycling bin.

Visiting Everglades National Park

Address   Everglades National Park
40001 State Road 9336
Homestead, FL 33034-6733
(305) 242-7700

Main Visitor Center

If you are coming from Miami, take the Florida Turnpike south to the last exit, then follow the signs to the park. For a treat, try a Key lime shake at Robert Is Here fruit stand, which you'll pass on your way to the park entrance.

Park Fees

There is a $5.00 entrance fee (which covers Shark Valley, too) for motor vehicles and a $2.00 fee for bicyclists and hikers. Golden Eagle, Age, and Access Passes are honored at the entrance station.

Facilities for the Disabled

The Main Visitor Center, just beyond the entrance station, which is open from 8:00 A.M. to 5:00 P.M., has a handout called "Accessibility" that will acclimate handicapped people to suitable park service facilities.

Length of Visit

A Few Hours to a Few Days: If you only have an hour or two to visit the park, head for Royal Palm Hammock. If you have a day or more, drive to Flamingo.

Campgrounds, Motels, and Places to Eat

Everglades National Park operates two campgrounds on the Main Park Road: Long Pine

Key and Flamingo. Both have RV and group sites. The Flamingo Lodge, run by TW Services, is the only motel in the park—102 air-conditioned rooms, 24 cottages with separate bedrooms and living rooms and fully equipped kitchens, a coin-operated Laundromat, and a screened-in swimming pool. TW also runs the Flamingo Marina, a gift shop and a restaurant with a view of Florida Bay, the Buttonwood Lounge, which serves drinks and sandwiches. Gasoline and limited groceries are available at the marina.

Boat rentals

TW operates boat tours into White Water Bay and Florida Bay and screened tram tours down Snake Bight Trail and rents canoes and houseboats. Rates and services vary with the seasons.

Address TW Services
Flamingo Lodge, Marina, and Outpost Resort
Flamingo, FL 33030
(305) 253-2241 or (813) 695-3101
For reservations only call (800) 600-3813

Chekika

There is a $4.00 entrance fee. The entrance is located 6 miles west of Krome Avenue (State Road 997) on Richard Street (SW 168 Street), north of Homestead. The 640-acre site was added to the national park in 1991 and is a good stop between Flamingo and Shark Valley. Facilities: a 20-site campground (one group site) will soon open; hiking trail, boardwalk through sawgrass, picnicking.

Shark Valley

ENTRANCE: Located on the Tamiami Trail 25 miles west of the Florida Turnpike exit for SW Eighth Street.

Park fees

There is a $4.00 entrance fee (which can be applied toward the Main Park Road if you continue on to the Homestead/Florida City station). There is a motel and restaurants on the nearby Miccosukee Reservation. For National Park Service information call, (305) 221-8776. For concession information regarding bicycle rentals and tram tours:

Address Shark Valley Tram Tours
P.O. Box 1729
Tamiami Station
Miami, FL 33144-1729
(305) 221-8455

Everglades City

GULF COAST RANGER STATION: 4.8 miles south
of the Tamiami Trail on S.R. 29. For park information call (813) 695-3311. There are private
campgrounds, motels, and bed-and-breakfasts.
For concession information regarding boat
tours and canoe rentals, contact:

Address Everglades National Park Boat Tours
P.O. Box 119
Everglades City, FL 33929
(813) 695-2591 or (800) 445-7724 in Florida

Visiting Big Cypress National Preserve and Vicinity

The Oasis Visitor Center

On the Tamiami Trail in Ochopee, 21 miles east of S.R. 29 and 37 miles west of Krome Avenue. There are no restaurants or lodging on the preserve. The nearest food facilities are 21 miles west of Oasis. Nearest lodging is Shark Valley to the east and Everglades City heading west. The nearest campground is in Ochopee.

Address Big Cypress National Preserve
HCR 61, Box 11
Ochopee, FL 33943
(813) 695-2000 headquarters
(813) 695-4111

Fakahatchee Strand State Preserve's

Big Cypress Bend is a 2,000-foot-long boardwalk into an striking stand of old growth cypress off the Tamiami Trail, 7 miles west of the S.R. 29 turnoff for Everglades City. See map 4 for details to W. J. Janes Memorial Drive.

Address   Fakahatchee Strand State Preserve
P.O. Box 548
Copeland, FL 33926
(813) 695-4593

Collier-Seminole State Park

Not within the scope of this book, but it offers fine camping (hot-water showers) and an easy drive to Fakahatchee, Big Cypress, and Everglades City. The park entrance is on the Tamiami Trail, 15.6 miles west of S.R. 29, or 8.4 miles east of S.R. 951 in Naples (an exit off U.S. 75). Reservations can be made sixty days in advance; rates are about $15.00 a night during the winter. Tents and RV hookups.

Address   Collier-Seminole State Park
Route 4, Box 848
Naples, FL 33961
(813) 394-3397

Checklist of birds that can be found fairly easily during the dry season (November–April) in the Everglades National Park

Key to Location Symbols Used

AT Anhinga Trail
EP Eco Pond
FB Florida Bay
PL Pinelands
MH Mahogany Hammock
C   Flamingo Campground
SV Shark Valley

- ☐ Anhinga AT, EP, SV
- ☐ American bittern SV
- ☐ Least bittern EP, SV
- ☐ Red-winged blackbird EP, C, SV
- ☐ Painted bunting EP
- ☐ Northern cardinal AT, PL
- ☐ American coot EP
- ☐ Double-crested cormorant AT, EP, FB, SV
- ☐ American crow AT, PL, MH, EP, C, SV
- ☐ Dunlin C, FB
- ☐ Bald eagle MH, FB
- ☐ Cattle egret C
- ☐ Great egret AT, EP, SV
- ☐ Reddish egret FB
- ☐ Snowy egret EP, SV
- ☐ Great-crested flycatcher MH
- ☐ Purple gallinule AT, SV
- ☐ Blue gray gnatcatcher MH
- ☐ Marbled godwit FB
- ☐ Boat-tailed grackle EP, SV
- ☐ Pied-billed grebe EP
- ☐ Laughing gull C, FB
- ☐ Ring-billed gull C, FB
- ☐ Red-shouldered hawk AT, PL, MH, EP, C, SV
- ☐ Great blue heron AT, EP, SV
- ☐ Great blue heron (white phase) C, FB
- ☐ Green-backed heron AT, EP, SV
- ☐ Little blue heron AT, EP, FB, SV
- ☐ Tricolored heron AT, EP, SV
- ☐ Glossy ibis EP, SV
- ☐ White ibis AT, FB, C, EP, SV

315

- ☐ Blue jay AT, PL
- ☐ Kestrel PL
- ☐ Belted kingfisher MH, SV
- ☐ Limpkin SV
- ☐ Eastern meadowlark MH, SV
- ☐ Red-breasted merganser EP, FB
- ☐ Northern mockingbird AT MH, EP, C
- ☐ Common moorhen AT, EP, SV
- ☐ Black-crowned night heron FB
- ☐ Yellow-crowned night heron SV
- ☐ Osprey AT, EP, FB
- ☐ Barred owl MH
- ☐ Great horned owl PL
- ☐ American white pelican FB
- ☐ Brown pelican FB
- ☐ Wilson's plover C, FB
- ☐ Clapper rail EP
- ☐ Least sandpiper C, FB
- ☐ Western sandpiper C, FB
- ☐ Black skimmer C, FB
- ☐ Sora EP, SV
- ☐ Roseate spoonbill FB
- ☐ Wood stork SV
- ☐ Tree swallow EP, C, SV
- ☐ Blue-winged teal EP
- ☐ Caspian tern SV
- ☐ Forster's tern C, FB
- ☐ Royal tern C, FB
- ☐ Ruddy turnstone C, FB
- ☐ White-eyed vireo AT, MH, SV
- ☐ Black vulture AT, EP, C, FB, SV
- ☐ Turkey vulture AT, EP, C, FB, SV
- ☐ Palm warbler AT, C, SV
- ☐ Pine warbler PL
- ☐ Prairie warbler C, FB
- ☐ Yellow warbler FB
- ☐ Yellow-throated warbler AT, EP, SV
- ☐ Willet C, FB
- ☐ Pileated woodpecker PL, MH
- ☐ Carolina wren AT, MH
- ☐ Common yellowthroat AT, EP, SV

Checklist of native reptiles of southern Florida

Crocodilians
- ☐ American alligator
- ☐ American crocodile

Turtles
- ☐ Peninsula cooter
- ☐ Atlantic loggerhead
- ☐ Stinkpot
- ☐ Diamondback terrapin
- ☐ Gopher tortoise
- ☐ Atlantic green turtle
- ☐ Atlantic hawksbill turtle
- ☐ Box turtle
- ☐ Florida chicken turtle
- ☐ Florida mud turtle
- ☐ Florida red-bellied turtle
- ☐ Florida softshell turtle
- ☐ Snapping turtle
- ☐ Striped mud turtle

Lizards
- ☐ Green anole
- ☐ Reef gecko
- ☐ Eastern glass lizard
- ☐ Eastern slender glass lizard
- ☐ Island glass lizard
- ☐ Scrub lizard
- ☐ Six-lined racerunner
- ☐ Ground skink
- ☐ Mole (red-tailed) skink
- ☐ Southeastern five-lined skink

Snakes
- ☐ Eastern coachwhip
- ☐ Common kingsnake
- ☐ Scarlet kingsnake
- ☐ Water moccasin
- ☐ Black racer
- ☐ Eastern diamondback rattlesnake
- ☐ Pigmy rattlesnake
- ☐ Brown (Dekay) snake
- ☐ Brown water snake
- ☐ Corn snake
- ☐ Eastern coral snake
- ☐ Eastern hognose snake
- ☐ Eastern mud snake

- ☐ Florida water snake
- ☐ Garter snake
- ☐ Green water snake
- ☐ Indigo snake
- ☐ Mangrove water snake
- ☐ Peninsula crowned snake
- ☐ Ribbon snake
- ☐ Ringneck snake
- ☐ Rough green snake
- ☐ Scarlet snake
- ☐ Striped crayfish snake
- ☐ Swamp snake
- ☐ Yellow rat snake

Checklist of amphibians of southern Florida

Salamanders
- ☐ Amphiuma
- ☐ Eastern newt
- ☐ Dwarf siren
- ☐ Greater siren

Frogs
- ☐ Chorus frog
- ☐ Little grass frog

- ☐ Pig frog
- ☐ Southern cricket frog
- ☐ Southern leopard frog
- ☐ Eastern spadefoot toad
- ☐ Narrow-mouthed toad
- ☐ Southern toad
- ☐ Green treefrog
- ☐ Squirrel treefrog

Checklist of native mammals of the Everglades/Big Cypress

- ☐ Brazilian free-tailed bat
- ☐ Evening bat
- ☐ Florida yellow bat
- ☐ Mastiff bat
- ☐ Black bear
- ☐ Bobcat
- ☐ Eastern cottontail
- ☐ White-tailed deer
- ☐ Atlantic bottlenosed dolphin
- ☐ Gray fox
- ☐ Manatee
- ☐ Mink
- ☐ Cotton mouse

- □ Florida mouse
- □ Round-tailed muskrat
- □ Southeastern myotis
- □ Virginia Opossum
- □ River otter
- □ Florida panther
- □ Marsh rabbit
- □ Raccoon
- □ Hispid cotton rat
- □ Marsh rice rat
- □ Least shrew
- □ Southern short-tailed shrew
- □ Spotted skunk
- □ Striped skunk
- □ Fox squirrel
- □ Gray squirrel
- □ Southern flying squirrel
- □ Long-tailed weasel

Checklist of common freshwater fish in the Everglades/Big Cypress region

- □ Largemouth bass
- □ Bluegill
- □ Bowfin

- □ Yellow bullhead
- □ Lake chubsucker
- □ American eel
- □ Florida gar
- □ Bluefin killifish
- □ Least killifish
- □ Marsh killifish
- □ Tadpole madtom
- □ Sheepshead minnow
- □ Mosquitofish
- □ Golden shiner
- □ Dollar sunfish
- □ Everglades pygmy sunfish
- □ Spotted sunfish
- □ Warmouth

Checklist of mammals, birds, reptiles, amphibians, and fish that are not native to the Everglades/Big Cypress region

Mammals
- □ Armadillo
- □ House mouse
- □ Pig
- □ Black rat

Birds
☐ Scarlet ibis
☐ House sparrow

Reptiles
☐ Bark anole
☐ Ashy gecko
☐ Turkish gecko

Amphibians
☐ Greenhouse frog
☐ Marine toad
☐ Cuban treefrog

Fish
☐ Black acara
☐ Walking catfish
☐ Mayan cichlid
☐ Pike killifish
☐ Oscar
☐ Blue tilapia
☐ Spotted tilapia

Checklist of common or easily found trees in the Everglades/Big Cypress region

☐ Sweet acacia
☐ Pond apple
☐ Seven-year apple
☐ Pop ash
☐ Willow bustic
☐ Buttonbush
☐ Buttonwood
☐ Bay cedar
☐ Cocoplum
☐ Wild coffee
☐ Eastern coralbean
☐ Bald cypress
☐ Pond cypress
☐ Jamaica dogwood
☐ Strangler fig
☐ Gumbo-limbo
☐ Dahoon holly
☐ Satin leaf
☐ Lysiloma
☐ West Indian mahogany

☐ Black mangrove
☐ Red mangrove
☐ White mangrove
☐ Red maple
☐ Red mulberry
☐ Wax myrtle
☐ Live oak
☐ Cabbage palm
☐ Paurotis palm
☐ Royal palm
☐ Persimmon
☐ Pigeonplum
☐ Slash pine
☐ Poisonwood
☐ Redbay
☐ Saw-palmetto
☐ Seagrape
☐ White stopper
☐ Sugarberry
☐ Shining sumac
☐ Sweetbay
☐ Tetrazygia
☐ Geiger tree
☐ Paradise tree
☐ Coastal plain willow

Checklist of serious plant pests in the Everglades/Big Cypress region

☐ Water hyacinth
☐ Melaleuca
☐ Brazilian pepper
☐ Australian pine

Further reading on the Everglades:

Carr, Archie. *The Everglades: The American Wilderness.* New York: Time-Life Books, 1973.

Douglas, Marjory Stoneman. *The Everglades: River of Grass.* St. Simons Island, Ga.: Mockingbird Books, 1947.

Lodge, Thomas E. *The Everglades Handbook: Understanding the Ecosystem.* Delray Beach, Fla.: St. Lucie Press, 1994.

INDEX